You Choose Books are published by Capstone Press
1710 Roe Crest Drive, North Mankato, Minnesota 56003
www.capstonepub.com

Library of Congress Cataloging-in-Publication Data
Names: Hoena, B. A., author.
Title: Could you escape a deserted island? : an interactive survival
    adventure / by Blake Hoena.
Description: North Mankato, Minnesota : Capstone Press, [2020] | Series: You
    choose: can you escape? | Summary: When an adventure at sea goes awry, the
    reader's choices determine if survival is possible for two friends
    marooned on a desert island with a deflated raft and few supplies.
Identifiers: LCCN 2019006000| ISBN 9781543573954 (hardcover) | ISBN
    9781543575606 (paperback) | ISBN 9781543573992 (ebook pdf)
Subjects: LCSH: Plot-your-own stories. | CYAC: Islands—Fiction. |
    Survival—Fiction. | Plot-your-own stories.
Classification: LCC PZ7.H67127 Cq 2020 | DDC [Fic]—dc23
LC record available at https://lccn.loc.gov/2019006000

Editorial Credits
Mari Bolte, editor; Bobbie Nuytten, designer; Eric Gohl, media researcher:
Laura Manthe, premedia specialist

Photo Credits
Alamy: Travelscape Images, 80; iStockphoto: Alfaproxima, 84; Shutterstock: Alex
Kosev, 104, Andreas Wolochow, 92, Arnain, 25, balounm, 46, BellaNiko, 28, Dmitry
Sedakov, 77, frees, 4, Gabriela Insuratelu, 42, hanohiki, 69, Jack Nevitt, 63, Jag_cz,
10, kanvag, cover, back cover, Kira Volkov, 103, Lee Prince, 57, lidialongobardi77, 97,
Peter Turner Photography, 98, pics721, 35, Shane Gross, 14, Shchekoldin Mikhail, 19,
Sony Herdiana, 53, Space-kraft, 39, Sunny Forest, 89, Vixit, 6

All internet sites appearing in back matter were available and accurate when this book
was sent to press.

Printed and bound in the United States of America.
PA70

YOU CHOOSE BOOKS

COULD YOU ESCAPE A DESERTED ISLAND?

AN INTERACTIVE SURVIVAL ADVENTURE

BY BLAKE HOENA

CAPSTONE PRESS
a capstone imprint

TABLE OF CONTENTS

WHICH DESTINATION WILL YOU CHOOSE?

Map Key:

1. Atlantic Ocean
2. Caribbean
3. Bahamas
4. Iceland
5. Pacific Ocean
6. Aleutian Islands
7. Indonesia (Java)
8. Australia
9. Coral Sea
10. Cook Islands

ABOUT YOUR ADVENTURE

YOU are about to go on the adventure of a lifetime. The ocean is calling, and you've decided to answer. Will you sail the north Atlantic and see rocky cliffs and icy glaciers? Will you explore the Pacific Ocean and play in the warm sun and gentle waves? Or is a trip to the great Land of Down Under in your future? But don't get too excited—you're about to be grounded on an island that only you can escape.

Every decision you make can lead you toward success or crushing failure. Make the right choice and survive. One wrong choice can mean injury, death, or the risk of never being rescued. YOU CHOOSE how your adventure ends. Pick wisely!

Turn the page to begin your adventure.

Chapter 1

SETTING OFF ON AN ADVENTURE

You have always wanted to travel overseas, and now you get that chance! You have been invited to go on a once-in-a-lifetime nature adventure. It's a great opportunity to view some of the world's most remote and exotic places, and observe wild animals in their natural habitats. What an exciting opportunity!

But before you start packing for your excursion, you need to choose a destination. There are countless places around the globe to explore. What interests you? Where will you go? What will you see? There are so many choices!

Turn the page.

You could sail the Atlantic. Northern Europe, with its countless fjords and many cultures, is just on the other side of the ocean. You would be able to see and explore places you've only read about in textbooks.

You could go island hopping in the Caribbean and visit sea turtle nesting grounds and enjoy warm, sandy beaches.

The Pacific has many exciting possibilities. Cruising the northern parts of the ocean to see glaciers and go whale watching would be an amazing experience. You'd be like an explorer out of a history book, breaking through the ice for the first time.

But southeastern Asia has numerous islands overflowing with different cultures. It is also home to some of the rarest animals on Earth.

The Great Barrier Reef and Marae Moana are two of the largest wildlife sanctuaries in the world. Both destinations are near Australia and can be reached by either boat or seaplane. Either place would be an adventure just getting there.

Which of the following adventures will you choose?

To sail across the Atlantic, turn to page 11.

To cruise the Pacific on a passenger ship, turn to page 47.

To fly to an Australian destination, turn to page 81.

Chapter 2

SAILING THE ATLANTIC OCEAN

Exploring the Atlantic sounds like the perfect adventure, you think as you enter the harbor. Your friend, Sam, and his dad wave to you.

They introduce you to the man leading your trip, Cap'n Bill. His ship, the *Moira*, is a 35-foot sloop. Aboard a small boat, you'll be able to get to out-of-the-way places.

Cap'n Bill shows you to the ship's galley. It is a cramped little room, but there is a cookstove, a sink, and a table for you all to sit around. Bunks and a bathroom are in the far back of the cabin.

"I've sailed this boat myself, to all parts of the Atlantic," Cap'n Bill says. "But it will be nice to have a crew on this voyage."

Turn the page.

He means you, Sam, and Sam's dad. As part of your adventure, you will get to learn the ins and outs of sailing.

Cap'n Bill pulls out a chart of the ocean and spreads it across the table.

"Before I can ready the boat," he says, "I need to know where you'd like to venture."

Sam leans over the map with you.

"What do you think?" his dad asks.

"We could sail south, somewhere warm, like the Caribbean," Sam says. "Or we could go north. Maybe head to Iceland, where there are active volcanos."

Both places sound like a lot of fun, but which destination would you prefer?

To get some sun, go to page 13.
To explore the north, turn to page 18.

"Let's go somewhere warm," you say. "We can hit the beaches."

"Only if we can go snorkeling while we're there," your friend says. "Maybe we'll see some sea turtles or stingrays."

After prepping his boat and gathering the needed supplies, Cap'n Bill is ready to set sail. You head southwest, along the coast of the United States. The shoreline stretches out to starboard.

During the trip, Cap'n Bill teaches you all there is to know about the *Moira*. He starts with port and starboard (left and right). That's the easiest part. How to rig sails and tie sailing knots takes some practice. Chart reading and navigation are even harder. You also learn important sailboat tips, like wearing a life vest and keeping yourself tethered to a safety line in rough seas.

Turn the page.

After reaching Florida, you sail southeast, skirting along the Bahamas.

"If you want to see sea turtles," Cap'n Bill says, "we can visit a turtle sanctuary."

You can't wait!

Four of the world's seven species of sea turtle live in the Bahamas.

But the ocean has other ideas. One night, you wake as the rocking of the boat nearly dumps you out of your bunk. You go above deck to see what's happening.

Lightning crackles across the sky. Thunder booms. Waves slam against the Moira's hull. Gusts of wind whip the sails about.

Cap'n Bill and Sam's dad are struggling with the rigging. You strap on a life vest and rush over to help.

"Don't forget your tether!" Cap'n Bill shouts. But his warning comes too late.

A huge wave washes over the deck. Sam's dad loses his footing, but his tether is clipped to the boat's safety lines. It keeps him from going overboard.

Turn the page.

You're not so lucky. As you reach for your tether, the wave sweeps your feet out from under you. You are tossed into the roiling sea.

Water surrounds you. You pull the chords on your life vest and it inflates.

In the dark, you hear Cap'n Bill shout your name. But you have no idea where he is. Heavy rain blinds you. Currents spin you about until you're dizzy.

You struggle against the waves, trying to keep your head above the water. You pass out from exhaustion sometime in the middle of the night.

When you wake, you are lying face down in the sand. You are wet and sore, and you have no idea where you are. But at least you are alive, and the warm sun is high in the sky and drying out your clothing.

Glancing up and down the beach, you see debris strewn about. You don't know if it's from the *Moira* or if Sam and his dad are safe.

Do you go looking to see if anyone else washed up on the island, or do you check out the debris littering the shore?

To look for other members of your crew, turn to page 22.

To check out the debris on the beach, turn to page 24.

"I've never seen an active volcano before," you say. "And how cool would it be to see one somewhere cold?"

"Agreed!" says Sam.

"Then it's settled," his dad says. "We'll travel the North Atlantic."

For a time, you sail northeast, along the coast of Canada. To port, you often see the shoreline stretching out along the horizon. But after making a stop in St. John's, on Newfoundland, you head north, across open ocean.

You sail to the southern tip of Greenland. The coastline is riddled with fjords, offering stunning scenery. These narrow inlets cut between the country's high cliffs. Even in summer, snow tops the mountain peaks. Miniature icebergs float in the water. "Bergy bits," Cap'n Bill calls them.

"Hope we don't hit a big one, like the *Titanic*," Sam jokes.

"Shh," you say.

Your journey takes you east, toward Iceland.

On your way there, you are caught in a storm. Winds whip at the sails, and waves rock the boat. Cap'n Bill has you go below deck to wait it out. But in the middle of the night, you hear a loud thud. A shudder shivers its way through the hull.

Turn the page.

Small icebergs are called bergy bits. Smaller chunks of ice are known as growlers. Larger pieces of ice are floebergs.

"Did we hit something?" Sam asks.

What happens next is a blur. Water starts flooding into the cabin.

Cap'n Bill shouts into the radio.

Sam's dad prepares the inflatable life raft.

Winds howl, and waves wash over the deck. You can hardly see as rain beats down on you. The boat sways back and forth violently.

In the chaos, you lose track of what's happening. You and Sam make it to the life raft, but you have no idea what happened to Sam's dad or Cap'n Bill. You wrap a rope from the raft around your wrist and hang on as best you can.

The next thing you know, it's morning. You find yourself lying in the raft. You've washed up onto a rocky beach. Sam sleeps next to you.

You are wet and shivering from the cold. Sam stirs as you get up.

"Where are we?" he asks.

"I dunno," you say with a shrug.

In front of you is a rough sea. Behind you is a steep rise up to a thick forest.

"Is the raft leaking?" Sam asks.

Looking down, you notice that it is not as inflated as it once was. That is when you realize you have little time to waste. You are in a cold, harsh environment. Your only way of escaping has been damaged.

What do you do?

To try to fix the raft, turn to page 26.
To try to build a fire, turn to page 29.

You are worried something might have happened to the *Moira* in the storm last night. Secretly, you are hoping someone else is on the island. You go in search of them. You do not want to try surviving on your own.

An expanse of bright blue sea stretches out in front of you. Inland, grasses, shrubs, and a few palm trees fill the horizon.

You turn to follow the beach. As you start around the island, you can tell it is not very big. The beach slowly circles to your right. But there are no signs of other people. And the farther you walk, the less debris you see.

While last night's storm was bad, your carelessness is the reason you wound up on this island. Everyone else is likely safe. It is probably best that you worry about yourself.

The sun is bright, and walking through the sand is harder than you thought. You're starting to sweat. That is when you look back inland and see trees and shade.

Hunger and thirst are starting to gnaw at you. You have not eaten since yesterday. You can't remember the last time you had a sip of water. There are probably coconuts up in the palm trees. But you do not know if there will be fresh water anywhere on a small island like this.

What do you search for first?

To search the ground for fresh water, turn to page 30.
To search up in the trees for food, turn to page 33.

Before running off to explore, you want to check out the debris. Hopefully you can tell whether or not it is from the *Moira*, and if anyone else may have washed up on the island.

There's not as much useful debris as you thought there would be. There are plastic bottles all over. You could store water in those. You also see pieces of driftwood. But almost everything else is just trash. While there are more items strewn about, none of it really looks like it came from the *Moira*. Seeing so much junk washed up on shore makes you sad.

Sam, his dad, and Cap'n Bill are probably all safe aboard the sailboat. Hopefully they have the Coast Guard looking for you.

It is estimated that around 8 million tons (7.3 metric tons) of plastic ends up in the ocean every year.

While standing there, your stomach rumbles. You have not eaten since yesterday. You saw coconuts in some trees that you could eat. But you also know that you need to work on a signal for rescuers to find you.

To search the island for food, turn to page 33.

To work on a signal for help, turn to page 38.

The raft got you here. Maybe it can aid in your escape. At the very least you could use it to sail around the island and hopefully find other people. Even small islands have lighthouses or other buildings you can use for shelter.

"We need the raft to survive," you say to Sam. "We'd better fix it."

Working together, you are able to pinpoint a small puncture. While exploring, you find an emergency pack. Digging through the pack, you find food and water. Some flares and a first aid kit are found in one of the pockets. There is also a patch kit. You are in luck!

You set to work, but quickly you begin to struggle. You have difficulty opening the patch kit. And then you keep dropping things. It is as if your fingers do not want to do what you are telling them to.

Sam tries to help, but he struggles too.

"I just can't stop shivering," he says between chattering teeth.

Your clothes are still wet, and every breeze seems to chill your bones. But you continue to work. Or at least you try.

What you do not realize is that hypothermia is setting in. It is getting difficult for you and Sam to think clearly. Both of you also find it tough to use your hands. When Sam stands to stretch his legs, he almost topples over.

When you finally realize how cold you are, it is too late. You find matches in the emergency pack, but you are shaking too much to light one. Several are wasted as you clumsily drop them onto the ground. You also don't have the strength to gather firewood.

Turn the page.

Greenland's Arctic climate means temperatures rarely reach above 50 degrees Fahrenheit (10 degrees Celsius).

You and Sam huddle together for warmth, but nothing can stop the uncontrollable shivering. First your friend, and then you, lose consciousness, never to wake again.

THE END

To follow another path, turn to page 9.
To learn more about survival situations, turn to page 99.

You are wet and cold, and you see that Sam is shivering. You realize that you need to dry out your clothes and get warm.

You look into the raft. There is an emergency pack, and you dig through it. Among the supplies you find food, water, and waterproof matches.

You and Sam then climb up to the forest and scrounge around for fallen branches and dry leaves. Both of you are shivering uncontrollably by the time you get a fire started. It is good that you got it going when you did.

Once your clothes are dry, you begin to worry about what you need to do next. You have food and water, but only enough to last a few days. You could go in search of rescue, or you could work on signaling for help.

To signal for help, turn to page 32.
To search for help, turn to page 35.

You know that you can survive many days without food. But water is another story. You have been out in the salty ocean, and now under the hot sun. Your throat is dry. Water is the most important thing to find.

There is a lot of vegetation growing out of the island's sandy soil. There must be water somewhere. But no matter how hard you look, you can't find any source of water.

By midday, the heat is unbearable. You rest in the shade of a palm tree.

That is when you see the green shell of a coconut hidden under some grass. You know there is food inside the shell. But what is more important is that there is also coconut water.

The coconut's outer shell is hard. You smack it against a tree until it cracks open. Immediately, sweet coconut water begins to leak from it. You lift the coconut above your head and let the clear liquid drip into your mouth.

Afterward, you finish breaking the coconut open and dig out the meat. There is not much, but at least it makes you feel a little less hungry.

Refreshed, you are now set to take on the task of making a signal for help. You walk back to where you saw the debris earlier.

Turn to page 38.

You have no idea where you are. In one direction you have an expanse of ocean. In the other direction, you have the beach, which is edged by a steep, forested slope. Neither are ideal. You worry about traveling around in an unknown place.

"It is probably best to set up some sort of signal," you tell Sam. "Search crews could be looking for us."

"But what type of signal?" Sam asks.

The beach is littered with rocks. You could use them to spell something out. A plane flying overhead might see it. You are also on the edge of a forest. Maybe you could gather more wood for a signal fire in case a ship passes by.

To use the rocks to write a message, turn to page 41.
To gather wood for a signal fire, turn to page 44.

Your stomach grumbles again. Food first. You set to work looking for something to eat. You remember seeing palm trees with green coconuts.

You stand at the base of a tree. It is a long way up to the top, and there are no branches to help you climb.

You pick a tree and hug it with your arms. Then you push yourself up with your legs. It is difficult work. The tree's rough bark scratches your skin.

The sun continues to beat down on you. Between last night's struggle in the ocean, trekking around the sandy beach, and now this, you are exhausted. You are incredibly thirsty as well. Your mouth feels dry. You are quickly growing weak.

Turn the page.

Halfway up the tree, you lose your grip. You slip and fall back to the ground. Stars light up your vision as you crack your head against something hard.

For the next few hours, you fade in and out of consciousness. You are hurt and find it difficult to move. Your lips grow chapped from the heat of the sun. Where are you? Eventually, you close your eyes one last time.

THE END

To follow another path, turn to page 9.
To learn more about survival situations, turn to page 99.

You do not know if anyone heard Cap'n Bill's distress call. And even if they did, how would they know where you are? You are stranded on an island in the middle of a great big ocean. The odds of being found by random chance are slim. You need to find a way to get help on your own.

"Let's fix the raft," you tell Sam. "Maybe we can find help."

Turn the page.

The Artic contains 94 major islands and 36,469 minor islands over half a million square miles (1.4 million square kilometers).

"There are probably people living somewhere on this island," Sam says, agreeing with you.

You saw a patch kit and pump in the emergency kit. You and Sam get to work repairing the raft. When satisfied with your work, you stow all the supplies from the emergency pack in the raft.

You hope to row around until you find help. Even small islands have lighthouses to warn ships of their presence. You could seek shelter there. There is also the chance that a ship might cruise by.

You row out from shore. As you begin to circle the island, the rocky beach slowly changes to a jagged cliff rising high out of the water.

The sea gets more treacherous. Rolling waves toss the small raft about. Waves splash you with water, soaking your clothes again. It is hard to row, or to even keep the raft facing forward.

"Maybe we should turn back," Sam says.

You begin to wonder if that would be best.

But before you can make a decision, a large wave pushes the raft hard into a rocky column. You hear a loud whoosh as air escapes from a hole in the raft. The raft deflates, crumpling into the sea. You try to swim to shore, but the steep, slippery cliff offers you no way out of the water.

The waves slam your body into the cliff. You have no idea where Sam is. You try to hang on, but your strength wears out quickly. Your fingers slip. You sink beneath the waves and drown.

THE END

To follow another path, turn to page 9.
To learn more about survival situations, turn to page 99.

You take a closer look at the washed-up trash. A sticklike piece of driftwood catches your eye. A shiny piece of metal shines next to it in the sand.

These give you two ideas. The metal could act like a mirror. You could reflect the sun with it, flashing light in the direction of an approaching ship or plane. Maybe that would get someone's attention.

With the stick, you could write a message on the beach. While a flash from the mirror might get someone's attention, the message would let them know that they should stop.

You set to work. With the stick of driftwood, you write HELP in the sand as big as you can. Once done, you sit down in the shade of a palm tree and wait. And wait.

Sometime in the afternoon, the buzz of an airplane's engine wakes you from a nap. You run out to the beach and stand next to the letters in the sand.

A small propeller plane is off in the distance, and not flying too high up. But you're not sure if they have seen your message.

Turn the page.

The United States Coast Guard spends more than 20,000 hours every year on search and rescue missions. Rescuers are located along the coastlines, island territories, and major lakes.

You pull the piece of metal out of your pocket. You point its shiny side in the direction of the plane, trying to catch the sun.

You know it works when the plane changes direction and flies directly over the island.

"Hey, down here!" you shout at the top of your lungs. "Help! Help!"

The plane turns around and makes one more swoop over the island. All the while you are shouting and using the metal to signal the plane.

While you doubt the pilot could actually hear you, you are pretty sure they saw your signals.

Help will be on its way soon, and you will have survived your adventure.

THE END

To follow another path, turn to page 9.
To learn more about survival situations, turn to page 99.

You discuss your plan with Sam over lunch.

"If we used rocks," you say, "maybe we could write a message that would be seen from above."

"Like 'HELP'?" he asks. "Or 'Save our ship'?"

"Yeah," you nod. "'SOS' might be easier since it's only three letters."

You set to work. It's harder than you thought. The rocks are heavy. You constantly get wet from the spray of waves crashing onto shore. And you continuously have to take breaks to warm yourself.

At one point, the fire nearly goes out, so you and Sam decide to take turns. While one of you moves the rocks around, the other searches for wood to keep the fire going. Everything is fairly wet, so you create more smoke than fire.

Turn the page.

By the end of the day, you are sore and exhausted. Your nose and eyes burn from the smoke. But after all your hard work, the rescue message is spelled out. Then, after stoking the fire, you and Sam lay down to rest.

You wake with water lapping at your feet.

The difference between high tide and low tide can range from 1 to 40 feet (0.3 to 12.2 meters).

You sit up, horrified to find that the water has crept up to where you were sleeping. What's even worse, the rocks you spent all day moving are now underwater.

"Sam, get up," you shout to your friend, giving him a nudge.

"Wh-what's wrong?" he asks.

When he sees the tide has rolled in, he shouts in frustration.

"I guess we should work on the signal fire," you say. You don't know what else to do.

Turn to page 44.

"All the leaves and branches are wet," you tell him. "They create more smoke than fire."

"That'd be great for a signal," Sam says.

"We just need to build it farther from shore," you say, sighing.

The slope of the island is steep, and you are constantly climbing up and down for fuel. By late afternoon, you have gathered enough branches. You hope you can attract the attention of any ships or planes out searching for you.

Later that day, you hear the buzz of an engine in the distance.

As Sam lights the fire, you grab one of the signal flares from the emergency pack. Between the fire and the flare, you have a thick cloud of smoke rising into the air.

A powerboat cuts through the waves toward you. You are saved!

From the boat's captain, you learn that Sam's dad and Cap'n Bill are also safe. Soon you will see them again and be able to return home.

THE END

To follow another path, turn to page 9.
To learn more about survival situations, turn to page 99.

Chapter 3

CRUISING THE PACIFIC OCEAN

Going on a cruise is totally your style. You might not get to visit as many different places, but it will be easier than sailing. You'll have more space to move about. There is a crew to run the ship and prepare your meals. You'll be able to observe your surroundings more fully.

Plus, it will be a super fun. Friends from school will also be going. It is a special class trip for students who are interested in studying the environment and wildlife.

One day, your teacher Mrs. Johnson asks students for suggestions about what to see.

Turn the page.

"We will be studying the wildlife around the Pacific Ocean," she begins. "We could either visit the northern part of the ocean, where we might get to see killer whales and visit glaciers. Or we could travel somewhere more southern, like Indonesia. There we could see some incredibly rare animals, like the Komodo dragon and the Sumatran rhino."

"What do you think?" your friend Jack asks, turning to you.

Both destinations sound thrilling to you. You have never seen killer whales or Komodo dragons outside a zoo. Where do you wish to go?

To cruise north, go to page 49.
To cruise south, turn to page 52.

"It'd be cool to come across of pod of orcas," you tell Jack.

"Or maybe some sea lions!" he agrees.

You vote. The majority of students select to visit the northern reaches of the ocean.

"Then it's settled," Mrs. Johnson says. "The weather in Alaska can be cold in early spring. Make sure to pack warm clothes!"

Your trip starts with a flight to Anchorage, Alaska. Next you take a train down to Seward, a small port town along the Gulf of Alaska. From there, you board your cruise ship. It's not exactly what you were expecting—there are no huge waterslides or onboard entertainment. It is a small ship, carrying less than 100 passengers. It leaves port and heads southwest along Alaska's coast. You sail toward the Aleutian Islands.

Turn the page.

Along the way, there are excursions you can take, like whale watching or helicopter rides over glaciers. You take advantage of as many of them as you can.

One day you sign up for a hiking excursion. Your view is beautiful, with a snow-covered mountain in the horizon. The coastline is a protected area for Stellar sea lions. You hope to catch a glimpse of some of the rare animals.

Somewhere in the middle of the hike, you and Jack wander away from the group. You were trying to get a better view of the scenery.

You get lost trying to find your way back to the ship. It is nearly dark when you find the dock. All the boats are gone.

"They left without us," you say, stunned. "Unbelievable."

"What are we going to do?" Jack asks.

You could wait where you are. Although it's cold, windy, and a little drizzly, people could easily find you. But there is no shelter. You might find better coverage in the nearby forest.

Which do you choose to do?

To stay near the shore, turn to page 56.
To find shelter inland, turn to page 58.

"Let's go somewhere warm," you suggest. "Then we could see all sorts of exotic animals, like orangutans or rhinos."

Mrs. Johnson asks the class to vote. "It's settled," she says. "We'll go to Indonesia."

After waiting several long months for your trip to start, you're finally on your way! The adventure starts with a long flight across the Pacific Ocean. You land in Singapore, an island on the southern tip of the Malay Peninsula. From there, you fly to Semarang, on the Indonesian island of Java.

The country of Indonesia is made up of thousands of islands. Java is one of the largest. There are several nature reserves to explore. You spend some time touring the island before embarking on your cruise.

The cruise ship is small. It holds less than 100 passengers. Instead of huge buffets and famous entertainers, it has a lecture lounge. Every day, you listen to naturalists tell you about the different animals you might see.

Turn the page.

Indonesia's 18,000 islands contain 10 percent of the world's plant species and 12 percent of all mammals.

The rest of the ship is just as cramped. You're sharing your tiny cabin with three of your classmates. When the weather is nice, you like to take walks on the deck. The cool air helps you feel less claustrophobic.

One night, you think you hear splashing in the water. You lean over the railing to see what it is. But you lean too far. SPLASH! You're overboard.

You yell for help, but nobody hears you. You try to reach out for a rope or a handhold, but the sides of the ship are smooth. There's nothing to grab. The ship glides past you, and then gets farther and farther away.

Throughout the night, you struggle against the waves and the current. Your only goal is to stay afloat. You have no idea where you are.

At some point, you pass out from exhaustion. When you come to, you are surprised to find yourself lying face down in the sand. Somehow you floated to the shore of an island.

You have no idea where you are, or what dangers might be at hand. But you do know that you will need water, and possibly shelter and something to eat.

What do you do first?

To explore the island for food, water, and shelter, turn to page 60.

To evaluate your surroundings, turn to page 67.

You are sure people from the cruise ship will come back looking for you.

"Someone has to notice we are missing," you say. "They could be back at any time."

You do not want to stray from the shore, even though it's cold, windy, and wet.

You wait. And wait. As the sun sets, it gets even colder. While you dressed appropriately to be hiking around during the day, you did not prepare for the freezing nighttime temperatures.

If you had the right supplies, you could try to start a fire. But you don't, and everything is wet. Even if you knew what you were doing, you would never be able to get a fire going.

You are chilled to the bone. You can't seem to stop shaking. All you can do is huddle together with Jack for warmth.

Alaska's shoreline is more than 46,602 miles (75,000 kilometers) long.

"I hope they hurry up," Jack says between chattering teeth.

"Me too," you say.

You drift off to sleep only to wake moments later. This happens over and over again. But slowly exhaustion overcomes you. You close your eyes and never wake again.

THE END

To follow another path, turn to page 9.
To learn more about survival situations, turn to page 99.

You have no idea if anyone has noticed that you are missing, or when you might be rescued. You shiver.

"We need to find some sort of shelter," you tell Jack. "We're going to freeze out here."

Jack agrees. Your clothes weren't meant for sitting in the rain after dark. And since you assumed you would be safe on the boat by now, you did not bring any supplies. Your only hope is to shelter yourselves from the weather with what you can find.

You and Jack walk into the woods. It's not really any warmer there, but at least you have some protection from the biting wind and the chilling rain.

"Maybe if we can find some branches," you say, "we could make a small shelter."

Trekking around is tough because of the steep terrain. You are practically walking on the side of a mountain. After a while, you and Jack stop to take a breather.

You hear the crack of a stick breaking. You and Jack look at each other. Neither you nor Jack has moved. You peek around the tree to see what made the noise. To your surprise, there is a large brown bear lumbering in your direction.

You have heard that bears can attack if surprised or threatened. How will you get yourselves out of this situation?

To run away, turn to page 62.
To walk away calmly, turn to page 63.

You have not eaten since the day before, and you remember just picking at the dry sandwich in the dining room. You also can't remember the last time you had something to drink. So you feel like food and water need to be your priority.

You won't find any food on the shoreline. Inland, a steep mountain covered by a thick carpet of jungle faces you. You venture into it.

It is humid and hot between the trees. You struggle to work your way through the dense foliage. Plants are everywhere, but you are not sure which are edible. You hear birds, and there is a constant buzz of insects. You could eat the birds, but you have no way to catch them. And you're not about to eat bugs—not yet, anyway.

For now, you decide to focus on finding something to drink. There are plants all over. There must be water somewhere.

Listening carefully, you can hear running water. You search until you find a small stream that runs from the mountain above. You give the water a taste. It is cool and refreshing. Success! You take a bigger sip.

Right away you feel better about your situation. But that feeling quickly disappears when you remember you're lost. You don't even know how to get back to where you started. You have wandered around quite a lot to get here.

Maybe the stream will lead somewhere useful. But maybe you should play it safe and just go back the way you came. Which path do you take?

To follow the stream, turn to page 66.
To turn back the way you came, turn to page 69.

"Jack, there's a bear," you say softly.

"We have to get out of here," he says, his eyes wide with fear.

"I know," you reply. "So on the count of three, we are going to make a run for it. 1 . . . 2 . . . 3!" You both take off as fast as you can.

You hear a roar behind you. Heavy footfalls follow. They are louder with every step.

You dare to look back. The bear is almost upon you. Then you fall. You weren't looking where you were going, and you tripped over a root.

It's over. The bear's teeth sink into your flesh. The blinding pain is the last thing you feel.

THE END

To follow another path, turn to page 9.
To learn more about survival situations, turn to page 99.

You motion to Jack to look around the tree. His eyes go wide when he sees the huge bear.

"What are we going to do?" he asks.

"We're going to get up, and slowly back away," you tell him. "OK?"

You know if you run, the bear might think you are prey. And if your back is to it, you won't be able to see if the bear charges.

Turn the page.

Alaska is home to black bears, brown bears—which include grizzlys—and polar bears.

Jack nods, and you both stand. Then you slowly start walking backward, carefully watching where you're going.

"Talk to me, Jack," you say.

"About what?" he asks.

"Anything, just do it calmly," you reply. "We want the bear to know we're here and not threatening."

"Can I tell you how thirsty I am . . . and hungry . . . and cold?" he asks, stepping over a fallen log.

You see the bear off in the distance. It lifts its head at the sound of your voices. It sniffs the air. But it does not move toward you.

You keep backing away until the creature is no longer in sight.

Once you feel like you are far enough away, you breathe a sigh of relief. You go back to scrounging around for pine boughs to make a crude shelter.

"It won't be much," you tell Jack as you lean a couple branches against each other. You keep talking to make sure that if there are any other predators, they hear you.

"It just needs to keep us warm until someone arrives tomorrow," you continue.

"Do you really think they'll be back?" Jack asks.

"Mrs. Johnson will probably show up looking for our missing homework," you say.

"So," Jack says, "what are we doing with all these branches?"

To use all the pine boughs to make a windproof shelter, turn to page 71.

To use some pine boughs for the walls and some for a bed, turn to page 73.

Because of the thick jungle, you took a meandering path to find the water. You doubt you could retrace your steps even if you tried. You would probably just get more lost.

The stream flows downhill from a mountain in the center of the island. You believe it will eventually lead you to the ocean. And no matter what, it seems smart to keep the drinking water nearby.

The stream cuts a narrow path through the jungle. Bugs are still biting you and the forest floor is still thick and prickly, but it is easier going than before.

Still, you are exhausted by the time the stream leads you to a beach.

You take a moment to rest and think.

You're hungry, but you don't want to just rush off to look for food. You already know how easy it would be to get lost in the forest. And you don't know what else lives there. You will need to be careful.

You stretch out on the warm sand. The sun dries your clothes. At least you won't need a shelter to stay warm. But you could overheat. Although not the safest place, the jungle can at least offer shade and water.

Next, you dig through your pockets to see if you have anything useful. There's not much. All you have is some change, the nub of a pencil, some lint, and a soggy note from your friend Jack.

You're finally ready to get up and move. You poke around the beach and find some driftwood and a clear plastic water bottle.

Turn the page.

Your stomach growls again. It's harder to ignore. But you know you have to make your presence known on the island. By now your classmates will have noticed you're gone. There may already be people searching for you.

You use a stick of driftwood to write SOS in the sand in huge letters. Maybe a search plane could see that. But, you realize, a ship would not.

You look at the water bottle. It could be used to send a message. Then you look at the driftwood in your hand. Maybe building a big fire would be better.

To send a message in a bottle, turn to page 75.
To try to start a fire, turn to page 77.

You decide to go back the way you came. But it turns out that doing that is harder than you thought. You had wandered around looking for water. The thick vegetation makes walking in a straight line impossible. As you go, it only seems like you are getting more and more lost.

Turn the page.

It is important to pay attention and stay calm if you're lost in a jungle.

The more you walk, the more you sweat. Bugs bite your exposed skin. Vines and leaves scratch as you pass. You are thirsty again, and, even worse, you're hungry too.

Perhaps you should have stayed on the beach before rushing off into the jungle. You could have made a plan, or thought of a way to keep from getting lost. Maybe you could have found something to use to carry water.

You're too tired now. You don't have the survival skills you need for this island. You eventually manage to find the beach again. But you succumb to exhaustion and starvation long before help arrives to rescue you.

THE END

To follow another path, turn to page 9.
To learn more about survival situations, turn to page 99.

Your biggest worry is keeping the wind out. The chilly air seems to sap your body of all its heat and energy. You layer the pine boughs to make a round tent, with a small opening to crawl inside. You stack on as many as you can find.

Not bad, you think as you crawl in. For the most part, you don't feel the wind.

But as you lay down to sleep, you just can't keep yourself warm. The ground beneath you is hard and frozen, and there's no way to get away from it. Both you and Jack spend the night tossing and turning, trying to rotate which body parts are touching the ground.

Your memory of what happens next is a little foggy. You wake to frantic voices.

"They're suffering from hypothermia," one says. She sounds worried.

Turn the page.

"We'd better get them back to the boat," another says.

You are carried on stretchers back to the dock. From there, a boat takes you to the cruise ship.

The staff doctor on board gives you all his attention. After some rest, you begin to recover. But at the next port, Mrs. Johnson makes arrangements for you and Jack to return home. Your trip is over.

THE END

To follow another path, turn to page 9.
To learn more about survival situations, turn to page 99.

You and Jack lean pine boughs against each other to make a lean-to.

"Wait!" you say as Jack starts piling up more branches. He looks at you, confused.

"Feel the ground. It's frozen," you say. "If we lay directly on it, we'll still be cold, no matter how windproof our shelter is. We need the rest of the branches for a floor."

While your shelter is not warm and cozy, it is also not freezing cold. You are at least comfortable. You're both able to fall asleep.

The next morning, you wake to voices.

"Look, I see a shelter!" you hear Mrs. Johnson shout. "This way!"

Turn the page.

Your teachers and several members from the cruise ship help you out of your shelter. You are then led to a boat that will take you back to the ship. On the way, Mrs. Johnson grills you about what happened.

"I had to contact both of your parents to let them know what was going on," she says. "They've said you can continue on with the trip, but only if the ship's doctor says you are OK."

You know that when you get back to the cruise ship, all your friends will be interested to hear what happened to you. You will have an exciting survival story to tell. Wait until they hear about the bear!

THE END

To follow another path, turn to page 9.
To learn more about survival situations, turn to page 99.

In the movies, people put messages in a bottle. The ocean currents send them where they need to go. You know that's silly. But it also seems silly not to try. They have to work sometimes, right?

You dry out the note from Jack in the sun. Using the pencil nub, you write a short note on the blank side of the paper with your name and any travel details you can remember. You make the letters as dark as possible, in case they fade.

You stuff the note into the bottle and screw the cap back on. Then you toss the bottle out into the water. The waves slowly carry it away. It feels like hours before it disappears.

What you didn't think about is that you're in a foreign country. People do not always speak English. If people find your note, they may not be able to read it.

Turn the page.

Even if they can read your note, and even if they give it to the authorities, there is no way for anyone to know exactly where you are. You gave your takeoff and destination information, but in between those places are thousands of islands. It would take years to search them all.

Also, you think to yourself, *when was the last time you opened a bottle with trash inside?*

The realization that you have little chance of being found hits you hard. You never recover. For a few days, you're able to survive on water, bugs, and strange-tasting plants. But your will to live is gone. No one will find you for years. And by then, it's too late.

THE END

To follow another path, turn to page 9.
To learn more about survival situations, turn to page 99.

It sounds silly and hopeless to send a message in a bottle. A fire seems much more realistic.

But you have no supplies to make a fire. What you do have is a small piece of paper and some lint. You could dry them out to use them as tinder. And you should be able to find plenty of driftwood once you get things going.

Turn the page.

Being able to start a fire, with or without matches, is a lifesaving skill.

Having kindling and fuel is great. But what do you do without matches?

Your water bottle is clear. If you fill it up with water and place it in the sun, its curved surface would act like a magnifying glass. If you could concentrate the sunlight on the paper, maybe you could start a fire.

You use the pencil to draw a black spot on the paper. You learned in art class that dark colors absorb light. Then you set up everything in the bright sunlight.

As you wait, you organize. The lint is handy to feed the fire. You also gather some dead leaves and sticks.

It seems to take hours, and you almost give up hope. But when the sun is at its brightest, you get a whiff of smoke. The paper starts to blacken.

Slowly you feed lint into the smoking paper. When you see a small flicker of fire, you add the leaves and sticks.

You build up a bonfire there on the beach. Handfuls of wet leaves create smoke. A black cloud rises from the fire.

Rescue crews had been combing this part of the ocean all day. One of them happens to see your fire on the little island. They quickly land and find you.

As you're carried away by your rescuers, you watch your fire get smaller and smaller. Soon you will be able to rejoin your friends aboard the cruise ship. You will have an amazing tale to tell.

THE END

To follow another path, turn to page 9.
To learn more about survival situations, turn to page 99.

Chapter 4

A FLIGHT DOWN UNDER

Spring break is coming up. You're looking forward to lounging around and hanging out with your friends. But then your grandparents surprise you with a trip of a lifetime.

"Australia? Really?" you ask, amazed. You've been dreaming of seeing the ocean for years. And now you'll be visiting one of the most beautiful destinations in the world.

You struggle to contain your excitement. Finally, the day arrives. Your grandparents pick you up and take you to the airport. You've got a long flight to Sydney, Australia. Then you travel north, up the continent's eastern coast, to Brisbane.

Turn the page.

On the way, Grandma says, "Before visiting the Great Barrier Reef, we thought of flying over to Marae Moana."

Marae Moana is one of the newest marine parks in the world. It was established in 2017, and not a lot of people know about it yet. It sounds like a nice, low-key way to start your vacation.

The following day, you hop on a small plane. You fly east, over the Coral Sea and toward the Cook Islands.

High over the ocean, you feel a sharp jerk. An engine on the plane has stalled. The pilot announces that he will have to make a crash landing.

Where are we going to land? you wonder. All you see is blue.

What happens next is chaotic. Grandma grabs a life vest from under your seat. Grandpa helps you put it on. They assure you everything will be OK. You aren't sure you believe them. You hunch over in your seat, waiting for the plane's impact with the water.

You see stars upon impact. You hear a loud screeching sound. There is water everywhere. Your grandparents scream your name.

Then everything goes blank.

When you wake, you find that you are still strapped to your seat. Your grandma is helping your grandpa out of his seat. The side of his head is bleeding. There is a man across the aisle who is still buckled into his seat. You unhook yourself and then slide over to help him. He is groggy and limps heavily.

Turn the page.

You climb out of the plane. You were in the back half. The plane's tail is sitting in the water. A chunk of the plane's side is about 100 feet away, and partially sunk into the sandy beach.

"What happened to the rest of the plane?" you ask, looking around.

The risk of crash is higher in small, private planes than on commercial flights.

"I think it sunk," the man says.

You peer out toward the ocean, hoping to see the plane's rounded nose. But all you see is blue water stretching flat for miles and miles. There's nothing to see but ocean.

You have crash-landed somewhere in the Pacific Ocean. Later, you will take time to think about the other passengers. For now, you need to think about yourself and the people who are with you. What will you do to ensure your survival?

To gather all of the supplies you can find, turn to page 86.

To use the plane as a shelter, turn to page 88.

While Grandma tends to the injured men, you decide to gather supplies. You grab everything you can find, from bottles of water to seat cushions. You even find a lighter.

By that afternoon, you have a mound of items piled high up on the beach. You head back into the plane for one last sweep.

You set foot onto the plane and realize you were smart to take out as much stuff as you could. The tide is rolling in, and your weight is enough to make the plane's body gently shift back and forth. By the time you've finished your last inspection, water is starting to creep in. You hop out before your feet get too wet.

Looking at the pile of supplies, you know that you have enough food and water for only a few days. That doesn't give you long. You hope that the pilot was able to radio for help before the plane crashed.

"We should get settled before nightfall," Grandpa says.

"I want to find out where we are," the man you rescued adds.

To stay put, turn to page 91.

To explore the island, turn to page 93.

If you clear out the plane, you can use the body as a shelter. It will provide both shade from the sun and protection from the wind and rain.

While Grandma cares for Grandpa and the other man, you set to work. You pull out the chairs and anything that looks like junk. Any supplies you find, including carry-on bags, you toss in the back. You can sort through it later.

By midafternoon you are exhausted and sweating. It's hot. You decide it is best to take a break. You make a bed from the bags you've scavenged. Then you drift off to sleep.

Hours go by. You hear Grandma shouting your name, which wakes you. You thought she was shaking you. But she's still on the beach. You roll over to get up and find the bottom of the plane is wet.

Tropical storms can lead to extreme winds, flooding, and hurricanes.

While you slept, the tide came in. Large waves are rocking the plane. The sky outside is dark. Storm clouds are rolling toward you.

Some of the supplies you gathered are falling over the edge of the plane and into the water. You run after them. But the waves rushing around the airplane cause a rip current. You are swept off your feet and dragged into the water.

Turn the page.

As you fight the current, you crack your head, hard, against the plane's tail fin. You lose consciousness.

The two men are hurt, and unable to come to your rescue. Grandma tries to reach you, but the combination of the waves and the rocking plane are too much for her.

You drown, never knowing if your grandparents will be rescued.

THE END

To follow another path, turn to page 9.
To learn more about survival situations, turn to page 99.

The back half of the plane is partially submerged in water. It's useless as a shelter. But if a rescuer saw it, they would definitely come investigate.

You and Grandma help the injured men to the edge of the forest. At least there they have shade from the sun. While you're making sure they're comfortable, something catches your eye. It's a large, shiny piece of the plane floating in the waves.

"Maybe we can use it to signal for help!" you exclaim. Before Grandma can stop you, you're in the water.

You swim hard, avoiding debris and other things floating in the water. You don't want to think about those things. Finally, you reach the piece of plane. It's about the size of a kickboard. You grab hold and then take a moment to rest.

Turn the page.

In 2019 researchers discovered that shark attacks had increased over the past 55 years.

Suddenly, something hits you—hard. The metal from the plane slides across your hand, cutting your palm. Then you feel something rough brush your leg. A huge fin breaks the surface of the water. You panic and swim for shore as fast as you can.

The plane piece did make the perfect signal. Unfortunately, it signaled something deadly instead. You never make it back to shore.

THE END

To follow another path, turn to page 9.
To learn more about survival situations, turn to page 99.

You have no idea if anyone is even looking for you. It seems smart to get your bearings.

Before setting off to explore, you and Grandma get the two men under the shade of some palm trees. You want to make sure they are far enough away from the beach during high tide.

You've emptied the backpack you were using as a carry-on. Among the supplies you brought to keep yourself busy, you also brought an empty, reusable water bottle. That should be handy in case you find fresh water.

As you walk around, you see plenty of coconuts up in the palm trees. You try to climb one, but Grandma tells you to get down. You gather coconuts that have already fallen instead.

Turn the page.

You also gather a variety of plant leaves, flowers, and a strange greenish fruit. Some of them have to be edible.

When you get back to the beach, you use a rock to crack open a couple of the coconuts. You find a little coconut water in them, which you pour into the water bottle with mixed success. Then everyone shares the coconut meat.

You're still hungry. You try the flowers, and they're very bitter. You spread the rest of what you've collected out on the sand. The fruit has a rough skin that looks like large, green scales. The leaves look a little like lettuce—only shiny.

Which do you try to eat?

To eat the green fruit, go to page 95.
To eat the green leaves, turn to page 96.

You cut into the green fruit with a plastic knife you found on the plane. Then you take a small nibble.

"It kind of tastes like apple," you tell Grandma, handing the fruit to her.

She takes a bite. "It does," she agrees. "But I'd spit out the seeds, to be safe." You all share the rest of the fruit.

Between the supplies you found on the plane and the fruit in the forest, you have enough supplies to survive. One day, either a plane will fly overhead or a boat will sail by. By then you will have built a signal fire or written a message for help in the sand. You are confident that help will come soon.

THE END

To follow another path, turn to page 9.
To learn more about survival situations, turn to page 99.

You are not sure about the fruit. The skin looks like it would be hard to cut, and all you have is a plastic knife. The leaves seem like a quicker meal, and you're hungry. You roll one up and pop it in your mouth.

"Tastes kind of like dish soap," you tell Grandma, making a face.

"I think I will stick to coconuts for now," she replies, smiling back.

That was a good choice on her part. Not long after eating the leaves, you feel a cramp in your stomach. The cramps keep coming and each one is worse than the last. Your skin breaks out in a painful rash, and a fever sends both heat and chills through your body. The leaves were toxic, and while not deadly, they weaken you a lot.

The jungle is full of tropical fruits that can help you survive. However, there are also fruits and vegetables that may not be good for you.

Sick, you are unable to help gather more supplies. Gathering food is too much work for Grandma, especially in the hot sun. As your supplies run out, your party dies one by one from dehydration or starvation.

THE END

To follow another path, turn to page 9.
To learn more about survival situations, turn to page 99.

Chapter 5

THE RULE OF THREE

Most people who get stranded at sea are rescued within a day. The choices you make in that first 24 hours are crucial. A hastily made decision could make your chances of survival more difficult.

Before leaping into action, the first step is to assess your situation. What are the environment and weather like? Are there any immediate dangers you need to worry about? If not, then take an inventory of your supplies. Even things that seem useless could be helpful. For example, a torn-up shirt could be used to make a rope. A scrap of metal could be used as a cutting tool.

Once you have a clear idea of the situation you are in and the resources you have, then it is time to act.

The rule of three can guide you in determining your priorities. There are three basic things you need to survive: shelter, water, and food. Which is most important?

You can survive about 3 minutes without air or in icy water.

You can survive about 3 hours in harsh weather.

You can survive about 3 days without water.

You can survive about 3 weeks without food.

If you are stranded somewhere cold and wet, fire and shelter will probably be the most important. If your body temperature drops too low, there is a risk of hypothermia. This condition can affect both your physical and mental abilities to do even simple tasks.

When you set up your shelter, consider the location. A beach might seem the best place. It is clear and will give you a good view of the ocean. But in a tropical area, the beach can be hot and lead to dehydration. In cold areas, you will be exposed to to freezing water and high winds, which can make lighting a fire more difficult.

No matter the location, you can't forget the tides. If your shelter is too close to the water during low tide, it could get washed away later on. This is also true of any distress signals you may set up.

If you are in a more tropical location, fresh water might be your priority over shelter. Under normal circumstances, people can survive a few days without water. But that changes in places with intense heat, where you sweat a lot, or if you have to physically exert yourself. Dehydration can cause fatigue and dizziness, making it more difficult to complete tasks.

Searching for food is only something to consider once you have shelter and a source of fresh water. Most people are rescued before they even come close to the point of starvation. Finding food can also be a tiring task. Most animals are difficult to catch without the proper skills and equipment. You will also need a knife to clean them and a fire and tools to cook the meat. And it won't last long once you do cook it, so once it's gone you'll have to find more.

Finding shelter can be easy or hard,
depending on where you wash up.

Most islands have plenty of vegetation. But be wary of the plants you eat. Berries can be nutritious, but they also can be harmful. It is best not to eat them, especially white or yellow berries, unless you know for sure that they are safe. Do not risk eating mushrooms. They can be very toxic. It is also recommended to avoid plants with shiny leaves or those with leaves that come in groups of three. If you start eating a plant and it tastes bitter, spit it out.

Having and maintaining a survival kit is important when disaster strikes! What's in your kit will depend on what situation you might encounter.

There are many other useful skills you can learn for just-in-case situations. How to start a fire safely and effectively and how to use basic emergency supplies are good things to know. And having a survival pack on hand can never hurt. Remember the rule of three, and you'll start off on the right foot.

SURVIVAL SUCCESS STORIES

1704: Scottish sailor Alexander Selkirk had an argument with his ship's captain. The captain decided to leave him on an island off the coast of Chile. Selkirk had a musket, a hatchet, a knife, and little else. But he survived for more than four years on the island. He built a hut from trees and hunted goats for food and clothing. Today that island is known as Robinson Crusoe Island. Selkirk's survival story inspired the book by Daniel Defoe.

1914: The story of Ernest Shackleton and his crew is one of history's greatest survival stories. Shackleton set sail aboard the *Endurance*. He wanted to be the first person to cross Antarctica. But in January of 1915, his ship became trapped in the ice. Eventually it was crushed by ice floes and sank.

Shackleton and his crew dragged their lifeboats nearly 200 miles (322 kilometers) across an ice floe to open water. Then they rowed another 150 miles (241 km) to Elephant Island in the Southern Ocean. They suffered from frostbite, starvation, and thirst before being rescued in August 1916.

September 1921: Ada Blackjack, a native Alaskan woman, joined an expedition to Wrangel Island, which is north of Siberia. She was hired to serve as a cook and seamstress. The trip was supposed to last a year, but the team of four men only brought supplies for six months. Then the ship that was supposed to pick them up was unable to get through the packed ice around the island. One of the men fell ill.

The other men decided they would try to walk to Siberia to find help. They left Ada with the sick man. They were never seen again.

Ada cared for the sick man for six months until he died. She learned to hunt and build a boat. She learned to use the expedition's photography equipment and took some photos of herself in camp. She was rescued in August 1923.

1943: Future president John F. Kennedy was serving in the U.S. Navy during World War II. On August 1 an enemy ship rammed and sank his ship. He and the rest of the crew were able to swim to a small, uninhabited island.

Their food and fresh water lasted only a couple days. There was the added danger of being discovered by the enemy. Kennedy decided to explore some of the larger islands in the area. He met some natives who agreed to carry a message to nearby allies. Five days after their ship sank, Kennedy and the surviving members of his crew were rescued.

October 1952: Tom Neale dreamed of living on a deserted island. He got a ship to drop him off on an island called Suwarrow. He brought two cats and all the supplies he could find on short notice. Some buildings and animals had been left behind by previous residents.

Neale raised pigs and chickens and planted a garden. He lived on the island for 15 out of 25 years, leaving three times. He wrote a book about his life, called *An Island to Oneself*.

January 1971: Retired Navy officer and dairy farmer Dougal Robertson and his family set sail aboard the *Lucette*. They spent a year and a half traveling. But orca whales struck their boat near the Galapagos Islands. As the ship sank, the family crowded onto a 10-man inflatable life raft and a 10-foot (3-meter) dinghy called the *Ednamair*. Eventually the life raft sank and they were all forced to board the *Ednamair*.

Food and water ran out after a week. They collected rainwater to drink, and caught fish and hunted sea turtles to eat. The family was at sea for 38 days before they were found by a Japanese fishing boat. Dougal wrote a book called *Survive the Savage Sea* based on their experience.

November 2012: Fisherman Jose Alvarenga planned on a 30-hour fishing trip off the coast of Mexico. Ezequiel Cordoba joined him. Their trip began with bad weather that only got worse. A storm destroyed the ship's motor and global positioning system (GPS). Alvarenga used the radio to call for help, but the storm continued to grow. Then the radio died.

Alvarenga developed a way to catch fish without bait or fish hooks. The men ate jellyfish raw and drank their own urine to survive. Once they found a garbage bag full of old food, which helped keep them alive.

Cordoba died after two months. Alvarenga lived alone on his boat for another year before he floated past an island. He swam to shore and wandered through a jungle before finding help on January 30, 2014. He had traveled 5,500 miles (8,851 kilometers) across the sea.

OTHER PATHS TO EXPLORE

◈ When people are stranded alone for a long time, one thing they struggle with is loneliness. Survivalists suggest making a "friend" in order to have something to talk to. Go back and read through one of the chapters, but as you make your choices, make a friend. It could be something inanimate, like a coconut, or a bird you see fluttering around your shelter. Imagine having a conversation with your friend about each of your choices. How does that help you decide what to do?

◈ There are thousands of uninhabited islands around the world. Many of them were created by volcanic eruptions. Imagine you were stranded on an island that had an active volcano. How might that change your priorities?

◈ Even some of the smallest, most remote islands have inhabitants. What if you were stranded on an island with people who spoke a different language, had an unfamiliar culture, ate food you had never tried, and did not have everyday technology like smartphones or computers? What sort of choices would you have to make? How would you know if the natives were friendly, and how would you communicate with them?

READ MORE

Braun, Eric. *Fighting to Survive in the Wilderness: Terrifying True Stories*. North Mankato, MN: Capstone Press, 2020.

Loh-Hagan, Virginia. *Deserted Island Hacks*. Ann Arbor, MI: Cherry Lake Publishing, 2019.

Silverman, Buffy. *Surviving a Shipwreck: The Titanic*. Minneapolis: Lerner Publications, 2019.

INTERNET SITES

Build a Kit—Basic Survival Kit
https://www.ready.gov/build-a-kit

Survive Nature—Deserted Island
http://www.survivenature.com/island.php